The Sun
Patri(

'These are the times that try men's souls.
The summer soldier and the sunshine patriot
will, in this crisis, shrink from the service of their
country; but he that stands it *now*, deserves the
love and thanks of man and woman'
[Thomas Paine, *'The American Crisis'* 1776]

The 1798
Rebellion
in Antrim & Down

R.M. Sibbett

Reprinted from:-
"ORANGEISM IN IRELAND AND
THROUGHOUT THE EMPIRE"
[Thynne & Co., Ltd 1938]

GOLI Publications
The Grand Orange Lodge of Ireland
65 Dublin Road, Belfast. BT2 7HE
Northern Ireland
E-Mail: goli@orange.thegap.com

© The Grand Orange Lodge of Ireland 1997

First Published 1997

British Library Cataloguing -in -Publication Data
A Catalogue record for this book is
available from the British Library

Sibbett, R. M.
    The sunshine patriots : The 1798 Rebellion in Antrim & Down
    1. Ireland - History - Rebellion of 1798
    I. Title
    941. 5 ' 07

ISBN 0 9501444 6 0

CONTENTS

	Page
Introduction	4
Biographical Sketch on R.M. Sibbett by his son Wilfred	5
State of the North	9
Presbyterian Loyalty	10
The Leaders	13
COUNTY ANTRIM	
Antrim Attacked	16
The Rebels	19
The Royal Forces	19
The Battle	22
At Brookhill	24
Lord O'Neill	24
Fate of McCracken	25
Spread of the Trouble	27
Carrickfergus	28
COUNTY DOWN	
County Down	29
A Fiendish Act	29
Fight at Saintfield	32
Newtownards and Donaghadee	33
Portaferry	34
Ballynahinch	35
Camp at Creevy Rocks	37
The Military	38
Rebels March to Ballynahinch	39
Camp at Edenavady	39
Monro's Proclamation	41
Nugent's Advance	42
The Country Devastated	44
The March from Downpatrick	44
The Battle	45
Fighting Renewed	47
An Eye-witness's Account	48
The Losses	49
Nugent's Report	49
Fate of Monro	50
A Narrow Escape	51
End of the Trouble	51

INTRODUCTION

As we approach the bicentary of 1798 it is an appropriate time to present a balanced account of the events in the Counties of Antrim and Down, which led to the Battles of Antrim and Ballynahinch. It was a decisive time in our history, marking the beginning of an Irish Republican tradition and leading directly to the passing of the Act of Union in 1800.

The Protestants of Ulster were torn both ways. Some with idealistic notions of *liberty, equality and fraternity* and the 'Rights of Man' threw in their lot with the United Irishmen. Others felt that their only security lay with the British connection and they remained loyal to the Crown and Constitution.

From this traumatic experience and with the passing of time as the news of the atrocities against the Protestants of Wexford reached the North, the Protestants of Ulster discovered that they must draw closer together as they had more in common than they had realised. This the Rev. Henry Cooke called a 'second marriage'. It has proved indissoluble.

This reprint from the larger work of R.M. Sibbett "Orangeism in Ireland and throughout the Empire", is published by the Education Committee with the addition of several illustrations and the minimum of editing. The support and encouragement of many people are acknowledged. The Sibbett family for their support particularly Mr Wilfred Sibbett the last surviving son of R.M. Sibbett, who has kindly contributed a brief biographical sketch on his father. The County Grand Lodges of Antrim and Down who have undertaken to support this publication by accepting responsibility for the sale of a proportion of the print run. This publication is commended not only to those within the Orange Institution and tradition but to all who have an interest in the religious and political culture and identity of the inhabitants of this island of Ireland.

While this is an all too brief account of the events in Antrim and Down we hope that it may be an incentive to read further into the history of the '98 Rising. A more detailed account of the events in Antrim and Down can be found in "The Summer Soldiers: The 1798 Rebellion *in* Antrim *and* Down" by A.T.Q. Stewart (The Blackstaff Press 1995 - ISBN 0-85640-558-2).

Brian Kennaway
Convenor
GOLI Education Committee
March 1997

ROBERT M. SIBBETT 1868-1941

ooOoo

A Biographical Sketch by his son
Wilfred Sibbett

Robert Mackie Sibbett, was a native of Portglenone, County Antrim, having been born on 4th September 1868 in the townland of Killycoogan. He came from a humble background and attended Gortgole and Aughnacleagh National Schools gaining a love of learning and a thirst for education which he kept throughout his life.

He was a man of wide and varied interests, particularly in local history and farming. In the 1890's he travelled to America but returned to his native land and started his career in journalism with the Ballymena Weekly Telegraph, where he wrote some articles based on his experiences in America.

In 1897 he then moved to Belfast and took up a post with the Belfast News Letter where he remained until 1920. He also wrote for the Ulster Farmers Journal and then in 1921 he joined the staff of the Belfast Telegraph, where he remained until his death in 1941.

He was a member of the Institute of Journalists throughout his life, taking the post of Chairman in 1917 and in 1927 he was appointed one of the Minute takers at the trial for heresy of Rev. Professor J. E. Davey, in the Presbyterian Church.
He wrote several books:

> The Revival in Ulster - The Life of a Worker
>   - William Montgomery Speers (1909)
> Orangeism in Ireland and Throughout the Empire 1688-1828, in two Volumes (1914)
> For Christ and Crown
>   - A History of the Belfast City Mission (1926)
> On the Shining Bann (1928) (Reprinted 1991)
> Princely Ulster Pedigrees (1931)
> The Hermit of Seapark (?)
> Orangeism in Ireland and Throughout the Empire 1688-1938, in two Volumes (1939)

ROBERT MACKIE SIBBETT 1868-1941

R.M. Sibbett had a great love for his birthplace, Portglenone, and in a tribute to the area and the people he wrote 'On the Shining Bann', a history of both the place and the local families, in 1928. Because of the wealth of information contained in this book it has been in great demand, so much so that it was reprinted in 1991.

He belonged to York LOL 145 and Killycoogan LOL 1175, and was a member of the Historical Committee of the Grand Orange Lodge of Ireland. In 1926 was appointed Historian of the Grand Orange Council of the World. A deeply religious man he enjoyed covering the Portstewart Convention meeting every year for the Belfast Telegraph. At the time of his death Mr Robert Clyde, Chairman of the Convention Committee wrote of him: *"Mr Sibbett's reports of the Convention breathed a spirit of understanding and intimacy that exhibited a deep spirituality."* Sir Joseph Davidson, Imperial Grand Master said of him: "*He was an earnest and devoted member, imbued with true Christian principles*".

In 1909 he married Miss Minnie Gamble, daughter of Mr James G. Gamble F.R.I.B.A. Clerk of Works at the time of the erection of the Belfast City Hall. They had two sons and a daughter, Robert, Wilfred and Beryl.

On moving to Glengormley, he became an elder in Carnmoney Presbyterian Church, and was instrumental in the establishment of Glengormley Presbyterian Church when, with a friend, he started up religious services in the local 'Tearooms'. He remained a faithful elder and Clerk of Session of Glengormley Presbyterian Church to the end of his life. His wife Minnie was Organist in the Congregation for thirty-five years, from 1935 to 1970.

While on the staff of the "News Letter" he contributed a long series of articles for the "Belfast Weekly News" on the History of the Orange Tradition from 1688 to 1829. In 1914 these articles were published in book form in two volumes by Messrs Henderson and Company, the proprietors of the "News Letter" and "Weekly News", under the title of "Orangeism in Ireland and Throughout the Empire". This publication ran to Sixty Chapters, each probably one of the original series of articles.

In the 1930's the Grand Orange Lodge of Ireland took a hand in the proceedings and persuaded him to write a further Forty-three Chapters, bringing his narrative up to the year 1938, the 250th Anniversary of the landing of William at Torbay. An Historical Committee, which later became the Publication Committee, was set up and his final publication appeared, again in two volumes, with the same title as before, just on the outbreak of the Second World War. This was published by Thynne & Company Limited, London, and is not only 'out of print', but is rare on the second-hand book market. This is the only 'authorised and complete' history of the Institution to date. R.M. Sibbett lived only another few years after publication, dying on 23rd October 1941.

This reprint consists of the original Chapters 35-37, of the Thynne & Co. edition, dealing with the Rebellion in Antrim and Down in 1798. It is hoped that this reprint in this format will serve to stimulate an interest in the '98 in particular and Orange History in general.

He wrote with an understanding of the motives of the men on both sides and does not attempt to hide the terrible deeds committed by each. His respect for honourable men from different sides is something we should emulate today.

Wilfred G. Sibbett
Whitehead
March 1997

State of the North.

While the rebellion was raging in Leinster, and the conspirators in the South and West awaited the signal to take the field, the disaffected in Ulster were watching and working. In that province, the birthplace and stronghold of the United Irish Society, various influences contributed to the postponement of the rising. Those principally concerned became distrustful and alarmed when they heard of the cruelties perpetrated on the Protestants in other parts of the country while many of their leaders absented themselves, and their movements were closely followed by the military.

The chief cause of delay, however, was the progress of Orangeism. It had become a great power in every county throughout the North, and attracted the sympathy of the gentry, who recognized its importance as a loyal and defensive organization Many Churchmen had become initiated, and the remainder who were eligible for membership, but still stood aloof, were among the first to admit that the principles of the Institution had their whole-hearted approval. In the brotherhood were also to be found large numbers of Presbyterians, who had no hesitation whatever in repudiating the alliance that had been formed by some of their co-religionists. The Leinster, Munster, and Connaught rebels were, with few exceptions, Roman Catholics, instigated and led by priests, and everyone saw that the fight was not in the interests of freedom in the general sense, but for the supremacy of their own faith. South of the Boyne the war was emphatically sectarian, and waged with the avowed purpose of destroying not only all Protestants, but every vestige of Protestantism. These were the terms of the horrible Black Oath, universally administered, and they were expressed in thousands of cruel deeds.

In the North, the conditions were essentially different. The rebels there were a mixed body of Protestants and Roman Catholics, between whom there was no real bond of union, no real harmony of sentiment, no tie of friendship, and no feeling that could be called fraternal. It was utterly impossible in the nature of things that real co-operation should exist between them, for one of the parties, in view of the policy influencing its efforts, could never rest satisfied with equality. Those, moreover, who did not belong to the Church of Rome, were also divided among themselves on various matters, both political and religious. It is true that among them was a considerable percentage of Presbyterians, who, owing to a misnomer, largely consisted of Unitarians, but everyone thoroughly acquainted with the history of the period must candidly admit that various other Protestant denominations were more or less numerously represented in the ranks of the conspirators. The struggle of the Presbyterians had always been for liberty of conscience, and just legislation; but those of them who were drawn into the United movement had been influenced to interpret these demands according to French principles. They advocated violence as a means of attaining their ends, which were not liberty and equality, but revolution, slaughter, and confiscation.

Presbyterian Loyalty.

Against this no part of the community was more loud in condemnation than the regularly constituted and responsible authorities of the Presbyterian Church, and, in illustration of this, it is only necessary to refer to the Declaration of the: Synod of Ulster, published in 1793: "The Synod of Ulster," said that very influential body,

> "feel themselves called upon explicitly to avow and publish their unshaken attachment to the genuine principles of the British constitution—an attachment early inculcated by the lessons of their fathers, and since justified by their own observation and experience. As members of civil society, they deem it not inconsistent with their public character to join with the great majority of the virtuous and enlightened men, in this kingdom, in expressing their opinion that a reform in the representation of the Commons' House of Parliament is essentially necessary to the perfection of the Constitution, and the security and maintenance of public liberty. In seeking this reform, they will not be seduced by the visionary theories of speculative men, but, taking the principles of the Constitution as their guide, they will co-operate with their fellow-citizens by all constitutional means to obtain this great object, rejecting with abhorrence every idea of popular tumult or foreign aid."

Sir Richard Musgrave, though by no means inclined to be partial to Nonconformity, bears honourable testimony to the fidelity of the Presbyterian yeomanry. He says:

> "In the Counties of Fermanagh, Tyrone, Derry, and Armagh, there were fourteen thousand yeomen . . . and they are all so loyal and so well disciplined that General Knox, who

commanded at Dungannon, reported, in the summer of 1798, that he would risk the safety of these counties on their fidelity and bravery; and, much to the honour of the Presbyterians, three-fourths of them were of that order. Though the Presbyterians lay under a general imputation of being disloyal, it appears that a great portion of them were steadily attached to the Constitution, and were ready to draw their swords in its defence against foreign and domestic foes. After many minute inquiries, I could not discover an instance of a Presbyterian yeoman having violated his Oath of Allegiance; but many shameful instances of the kind occurred among the Romish yeomen in Leinster, Connaught, and Munster."

It is gross slander, then, upon Presbyterian loyalty to state that Presbyterians, as a body, were mixed up in the rebellion. No one, however, will deny that the conspirators who professed themselves Protestants, whether Presbyterians, or members of any other kindred denomination, hated King and Constitution hated the aristocracy and the country squire, hated the Church and State, and, in proportion as they hated these, loved Tom Paine and his Rights of Man. Caught by the glamour of a rationalistic creed, they had lost their old spiritual moorings. From one of their most popular songs, "The Hearty Fellows' Delight", one understands the recklessness characteristic of members of the United Irishmen:

> *"The mighty Thomas Paine,*
> *Who freedom did maintain*
> *With energy of reason and sense*
> *Was stupid as an ass*
> *Till first he took a glass,*
> *Then truth sprang from his cruiskeen lawn"*

Another song, which also enjoyed much popularity amongst the fraternity, was "The Rights of Men", which expressed admiration of the French and class enmity:

> *"Fame ! let the trumpet sound,*
> *Tell to the world around*
> *   Frenchmen are free.*
> *Tell ribbands, crowns, stars,*
> *Kings, traitors, troops, and wars,*
> *Plans, councils, plots, and jars*
> *   We will be free."*

The reunions of the Northern Whig Club had taught the leaders and the rank and file of the United Irish Society to drink such toasts as "Gallic Liberty", to regard the fall and demolition of the Bastille as an evidence of the progress of liberal principles, and to speak of the French Revolution as meritorious. Two verses from "Freedom Triumphant" explain the feelings of the Northern Rebels in relation to violent changes in society:

"On fourteenth of July in Paris town,
There was a grevious battle,
Where many a tyrant lay on the ground,
By cannon that did rattle;
The people firmly did advance,
Which made their foes to wonder
Their country's rights they did maintain
The Bastille tore asunder.
A standard then they did prepare
Liberty's stripes they raised
Which did inspire with electric fire
Frenchmen so long enslaved;
With sword in hand they marched on,
Their foes they soon did scatter;
Both tyrant, crown, mitre, and gown,
Their pikes that day did tatter."

What must have been the thoughts of a genuine Protestant - a Protestant unseduced from the pure principles of his religion and still mindful of the struggles of his forefathers on its behalf - who listened to the jingle of that composition, which is a parody on a song the most thrilling for him in the language. What also must have been the feelings of the genuine Roman Catholic, who heard the "heretic" by his side exult in the tattering of mitre and gown ! It is plain, from a calm survey of the situation, that the great motive force behind the rebellion in Ulster was irreligiousness, blatant infidelity resting here and there on the slow-smouldering fires of bigotry, ready at any moment to burst, as in too many cases they did elsewhere, into ungovernable and devastating flames.

The Leaders.

As a rule, the leaders in Ulster were men of good social position, and their education would have gained for them distinction had it been rightly employed. Archibald Hamilton Rowan was descended from an ancient Scottish family settled in Ireland from the reign of James the First. Born in London on the 12th of May, 1751, where his father, Gavin Hamilton, had gone to reside in the year 1750, he, after the death of his maternal grandfather, adopted the name of Rowan. He was a man of great physical strength, gay, and of daring character. As a private in his father's company, he took part in the last review of Volunteers at Belfast. He joined the Northern Whig Club, from which transition was easy to the Society of United Irishmen, and he got so intimately associated with the conspiracy fostered by the latter organization that he found it necessary to consult his own safety by flight. At this time he had been sentenced to two years' imprisonment for libel contained in an address; but he managed to bribe the jailer, and effect his escape. From Newgate, he crossed to France, and then proceeded to America. In 1806 he returned to Ireland, in full enjoyment of pardon, and settled in Killyleagh, where he died, esteemed and lamented, on the 1st of November, 1834.

Thomas Russell was born at Bessborough, County Cork, and educated for the Church; but chose a military career, and was appointed a captain of the 64th Regiment. He filled the office of Seneschal to the Manor Court of Dungannon, and was a Justice of the Peace for County Tyrone. Later, he acted as librarian, in connection with the Linenhall Library, Belfast, and contributed to the Northern Star. It would appear from some manuscripts concerning him that Russell, who belonged to the Established Church, was a loyal man, when he came to Belfast with his regiment, but, having peculiar notions about the Millennium, a few democratic families, whose acquaintance he had formed, persuaded him to believe that the United system would promote the introduction of that happy period, by helping to bring about universal peace. He was appointed to command the rebels in Down, but the Government interrupted his plans, and lodged him successively in Newgate and Fort George. Along with other leaders, he was sent out of the country, and escaped, in 1798, the punishment that befell him a few years subsequently.

William Sampson, a King's Counsel, was a man of a different type. Son of an Episcopalian clergyman, * he was born in Londonderry, and educated in Trinity College. He became an active United Irishman,

Henry Joy M'Cracken 1767-1798

and pleaded their cause in Court, while in the Northern Star and other publications he made foul attacks upon Orangeism. Like Captain Russell, Sampson was allowed to retire to the Continent. He afterwards sailed to America, joined the Bar, and rose to considerable eminence.

Henry Joy M'Cracken was born in Belfast, and held a respectable position in the linen business. He was the first to introduce cotton spinning to his native town, the earliest experiments in that direction being made in the Old Poorhouse. One of the founders of the United Irish Society, he was among its most faithful adherents. After being imprisoned in Dublin for thirteen months, he returned to Belfast, threw himself into the revolutionary movement, and held chief command at the Battle of Antrim, where his bravery was neutralized by the pusillanimous conduct of the second officer. He was arrested, tried by court-martial, and executed the same evening, at a place still easily recognized in High Street, Belfast. The remains of the unfortunate M'Cracken were interred in the old burying ground, which now forms the site of St. George's Church.

Henry Munro, educated an Episcopalian, was born in Lisburn, and he, too, was connected with the linen trade. He commanded the insurgents at Ballynahinch, and, when deserted by his force, fled to the mountains; but was captured, tried by court-martial, and executed before his own door. His widow survived until February, 1840, and, having seen more than enough of the foolish United Irishmen, showed herself on the side of loyalty by taking a keen interest in the 12th of July celebrations. Dr. William Steel Dickson was a Presbyterian minister, who identified himself with the "New Light" doctrines, which men who abode by the old ways, considered responsible for introducing lax views regarding the obligation of the Fourth Commandment. Possessing great energy of character, and a fluent speaker, he took a prominent part in electioneering contests.

When the Society of United Irishmen sprang into existence he allowed himself to be appointed commander of the rebels of County Down. He was arrested on the eve of the insurrection, and imprisoned in Fort George for three years. His subsequent career was unfortunate, and, according to one of his admirers, * "the remains of that great man were deposited in a pauper's grave, where not even a stone marks the narrow house of his repose". The Rev. William Jackson, an Episcopal clergyman, was the first to be convicted of carrying on a treasonable correspondence with the French. He was condemned to capital punishment, but poisoned himself to avoid the ignominy of a public execution. The Rev. James Porter, born at Ballindrait, County Donegal, was a prominent member of the United Irish Society. He took the field with the rebels at Saintfield, was tried by court-martial, and, notwithstanding earnest entreaties, executed in sight of his own church and home at Greyabbey. The Rev. Sinclair Kelburn, minister of the Third Presbyterian congregation, Rosemary Street, Belfast, " possessed," says Dr. Reid, " a considerable amount of popular talent, but he wanted decision of character." The late Rev. John Scott Porter referred to him as "a remarkable man in many respects, as an orator, a divine, and a politician; but it does not appear," said the same authority, "that he was ever connected with the Society of United Irishmen." His name appeared as one of the committee nominated to call together a convention at Dungannon, the result of a meeting of United Irishmen in Belfast, and he was associated with Wolfe Tone in that town. In Newgate he gave the United Irishman's password, "Up," in reply to an observation by Lord Carhampton. Dr. William Drennan, a Belfast man, was one of the most graceful authors of his day. His style in prose and verse is universally admired, whatever may be thought of the sentiments. He had no faith in the Whig Club, " whose members wore a suit of blue, with blue velvet cuffs and capes, and a gilt button with the motto, Persevere".

The Rev. James Simpson, of Newtownards; the Rev. Thomas Ledlie Birch, of Saintfield; and several other Northern leaders, clergymen and laymen, were also men of note, in their respective circles, who made a bad use of their energies and talents. The insurrection was not delayed in Ulster owing to any lack of courage, for all things were ready; but to the insincerity of the Roman Catholics, and the reports that came daily to hand concerning the atrocities these allies were committing in other districts where the Protestant population could only offer comparatively small resistance. Distrust spread on every side, and, in the end, brought total failure on the enterprise.

Antrim Attacked.

The first outbreak in Ulster occurred at Antrim, nominally the capital of the county of that name. In the year of the great Rebellion, and at other periods in the history of the province, dark deeds were done in and around that town, which now became once more the scene of deadly and cruel conflict. The same races were again engaged, but on one side descendants of old-time enemies were arrayed together, and

Antrim Town in 1798

Antrim Town in 1798.

A. Lord Massereene's Garden.
B. Where Lord O'Neill fell.
C. Where dragoons retreated across the river.
D. Churchyard
E. Col. Durham's Artillery Firing Point

Based on plan published in U.J.A. Jan. 1895.

from that point of view the situation was tragic. The folly of it was discovered soon afterwards, and before two decades had passed away the families of those who stood in the rebel ranks at Antrim on the 7th of June, 1798, were among the most enthusiastic in their professions of attachment to the British Throne and Constitution.

At the time referred to, little change had taken place in the town. The market-house stood in the centre of Main Street. It was a square building, supported by stone pillars, and, like Main Street, was commanded by the wall enclosing Lord Massereene's garden. A second wall, at right angles to the garden wall, and flanking it, commanded Bow Lane. A church stood about half-way between the market house, beside which was the guard-house, and the end of Scots Quarter, where the houses, erected on an eminence, were protected by a wall eight feet high. The Massereene Bridge was a short distance from Main Street. Antrim was in possession of the Royal forces, and the plan of the conspirators was to capture it. As a result of doubtful deliberations, it was decided that the rebels should take the field on the day mentioned, though their friends in County Down had declared themselves anxious for a postponement of hostilities until a more suitable moment. Henry Joy M'Cracken was chosen to command, Dickson and other leaders having been thrown into prison, and he was daring enough for the position.

On the 21st of May he had proposed heading an armed party to seize Colonel Montgomery and his officers, who were practically all assembled at a ball in the Exchange, Belfast. This project was, however, over-ruled, and he attempted the even more hazardous one which we are describing. It was known that a meeting of magistrates, summoned by Lord O'Neill, Governor of the County, would take place in Antrim on the 7th of June. The idea, therefore, suggested itself to the minds of M'Cracken and his followers to seize his Lordship and the other Justices, and secure the surrendered arms that had not yet been removed. Orders were issued accordingly. The general rendezvous selected was Donegore Hill, and instructions were given to surprise and capture small parties of military quartered throughout the county. These arrangements, made by a man without previous military experience, testified to considerable ability. Everything depended upon promptitude, and it was hoped that in a few days, not only Antrim, but Randalstown, Ballynahinch, Saintfield, Newtownards, and Portaferry, places of importance in those days, would be in the hands of the United Irishmen.

The Rebels.

At Antrim the plan of the rebels was to march in four columns. The first, from the district lying towards Belfast, was to enter the town by the Belfast road; the second, from Ballynure, Ballyclare, and Doagh, was to enter by the Carrickfergus road, and join the Belfast column at Scots Quarter; the third, from Connor, Kells, and Ballymena, was to proceed through Patie's Lane; and the fourth, from Shane's Castle, Randalstown, and Dunbilty, was to enter by Bow Lane. M'Cracken marched his column in three divisions. The musketeers were in front, the pikemen in the centre, and two brass field-pieces, 6-pounders, in the rear. Green banners waved over the centre of each division, and the men sang the French revolutionary hymn, Marseillaise, then enjoying much popularity amongst members of the Society. Although the day was sultry, the rebel troops swung along at a good pace, their weapons gleaming in the sun, and spectators, on the way, knew that trouble was fast approaching. Some in the ranks had parted with fathers, husbands, and brothers, whom they were never to see in life again.

When in view of the town, the commander halted his forces, and harangued them. The response to his words was, " Lead us to liberty or death." The attack by the first three columns was timed to take place at half-past two o clock in the afternoon, and by the fourth column, which was under Samuel Orr, a brother of William Orr, a few minutes later. A mishap, however occurred. About one o'clock several pikes were discovered in a garden in Scots Quarter, and the house was set on fire. The flames quickly spread, and affected several other buildings. Observing the fire, and not knowing the cause, the rebels halted for nearly half an hour. During the delay a dispute arose amongst the Roman Catholics in Orr's column and the Presbyterians. The former insisted that all the Orangemen in the town should be put to death, and the latter opposed, declaring that they would never consent to such an act of cruelty. The discussion eventually ceased, and the march was resumed. It was, however, abundantly clear that among these men going into battle there could be no real and lasting union.

The Royal Forces.

In the meantime, General Nugent, who had been informed of the intentions of the rebels, sent orders to Blaris camp for the second light battalion to march with all possible haste to Antrim. This battalion was composed of companies of the 64th Regiment, and of the Armagh, Monaghan, Dublin, Kerry and Tipperary militia, and one hundred and fifty men of the 22nd Light Dragoons, with two curricle 6-pounders and two five and-a-half-inch howitzers. Colonel Clavering commanded the militia, and the Honourable Colonel Lumley the dragoons. The General also ordered two hundred and fifty men of the Monaghan regiment, a troop of the 22nd Light Dragoons, and the Belfast Cavalry to march under the command of Colonel Durham from Belfast, by Carnmoney and Templepatrick. But these did not represent the whole of the Royal forces. Orangemen were at Antrim, as Orangemen; and there, too, were many yeomanry corps that had come from the camp at Blaris, where General Nugent had formed a thousand of such troops. In addition, the Magheragall Cavalry, under Lieutenant Garrett, accompanied Colonel Lumley from Lisburn, at his special request, while the chief officer of the corps, Captain Wakefield, with other yeomen, also at the request of Colonel Lumley remained to take charge of the home post, not the least important part of the general arrangements, having regard to the fact that the residences of many of the gentry of the neighbourhood were marked out by the rebel leaders for their own personal use.

Early in the morning an orderly galloped into Antrim, and informed Major Seddon of the intended attack, and the drums beat the alarm. Immediately the local yeomanry corps, the Orangemen, and other loyal Protestants, in all about four hundred men, presented themselves at the rendezvous, demanding arms for the defence of their homes. Arms, however, were not to be had, and, of the two hundred who declined to return to their homes, because of their anxiety to take part in the fight, only about eighty could be furnished with weapons of that character. The supply of ammunition also was very limited. Yeomen could only obtain twelve rounds each, while Orangemen and volunteers had to content themselves with seven rounds less. This was at nine o'clock. At ten o'clock news arrived that the rebels were pressing forward, with large numbers compelled to join them on the way. This was disconcerting; but, two hours later, amid the loud cheers of the little garrison, Captain James Stewart and Lieutenant Gamble, of the Dunseverick Yeomanry Cavalry, with fifteen men, entered the town from Ballymena, having cut through about two hundred rebels near Kells.

Battle of Antrim 7th June 1798

The Battle.

At three o'clock in the day, the rebels began the attack. By a singular coincidence, the assailants and part of the forces from Blaris camp entered Antrim simultaneously from opposite directions, the rebel columns appearing at the Scots Quarter as the advanced guard of the light battalion crossed the Massereene Bridge, and formed in Main Street. Advancing from the Scots Quarter about four thousand strong, the front composed of eight hundred musketeers, excellent marksmen, the head of the United column was within one hundred and forty yards of the bridge, when Lieutenant Neville, who had taken his post there with two 6-pounders, flanked by yeomanry and dragoons under Colonel Lumley, opened fire with case shot, to which the rebels replied with a 6-pounder that had been stolen from Belfast. But this gun soon became disabled by its own recoil.

The street firing of the attacking force was better, and while the pikemen were despatched across the field to take the Royalists in the rear, the musketeers went forward and took the churchyard. The order was then given to limber up, and Neville, with his two guns, retreated to another position, covered by a daring charge of cavalry by Colonel Lumley. The charge was brilliantly delivered, but it was indiscreet. The pikemen had formed in close column in Bow Lane, in rear of the military, and the dragoons, in order to reach this column, were compelled to pass the churchyard, within four or five yards of the rebel musketeers, who, protected by the wall, opened upon them a deadly fire. Notwithstanding this, the difficult task was performed, the brave troops, cutting their way through the rebel ranks, and charging back towards the churchyard wall; but their loss was heavy. Of the 80 officers and men who took part in the charge, which occupied about two minutes, Cornet Dunn and Lieutenant Gamble, Quartermaster Simpson, and seventeen men were killed, while Colonel Lumley, Major Seddon, Cornet Reed, and thirty men were wounded. The horses killed numbered about forty.

After this disaster, the yeomen and Orange volunteers retired and took possession of Lord Massereene's garden. Here they could command Bow Lane, and, in some degree, protect the guns under the wall, where a party of dragoons was posted, with Lord O'Neill and Rev. Dr. Macartney. The rebels continued to advance on Bow Lane, and were warmly received by the two guns. Colonel Lumley now thought it prudent after the losses he had sustained to order a general retreat; but the corps of Magheragall Cavalry, not understanding the call of the bugle, remained exposed to the destructive assaults of the United Men. Seeing what had happened, the Colonel exclaimed, " The poor fellows will be cut to pieces," and, galloping forward, led them out of their perilous position, receiving a second wound in the operation. The Royalists, then greatly pressed and, without reinforcements, fell back across the bridge.

At that moment Commodore Watson's horse leaped over the parapet into the river, and by so doing saved his master's life. Lord O'Neill, whose horse got injured and became restive, was dragged to the ground by a pikeman, and mortally wounded. Dr. Macartney, cutting his way through the rebels, managed to escape; but, being unable to overtake the dragoons, he joined Mr. Staples, member for the county, crossed Lough Neagh in a row boat, and hurriedly described to General Knox at Dungannon what had occurred. Acting promptly on the information, the General assembled all the yeomanry of that part of the country, numbering fifteen hundred, and marched with them to Toome, in order to prevent the rebels of County Derry rising and co-operating with the Antrim insurgents.

On the retreat of the dragoons, the United men, flushed with success, rushed forward with a horrid yell, and seized the curricle guns; but every man of the party that made the rush was shot by the yeomen, while the remainder of the column retreated. Presently, Lieutenant John Macartney, of the Antrim Yeomanry, assisted by his brother, Lieutenant Arthur Macartney - both sons of Rev. Dr. Macartney, and under twenty years of age made a sally from a garden with twenty of the Antrim corps, drew up the guns on the ammunition cart, and, having planted them on the wall, scattered the rebels with a few discharges of round shot. They, however, re-formed at several places round the town to renew the assault. Matters at this stage looked somewhat gloomy for the Royalists; but Colonel Orr, frightened at the report of the guns, precipitately retreated at the head of his column, fifteen hundred strong, to Randalstown. That act, variously explained, but said by friends of the Colonel to be due to the opinion he had formed as to the hollowness of the alliance between the men under him, and the impossibility of conducting a government that would satisfy all, proved the turning point in the battle. It neutralized the splendid efforts of M'Cracken, and, although a second attack was in contemplation, that leader soon became convinced of its futility. Reinforcements from Belfast and Blaris had arrived, and the task before the rebels was one of vastly increased difficulty. The United Irishmen, feeling that they could no longer entertain hopes of success, quickly allowed their minds to fall into a despairing mood, and in a few minutes they were running in all directions. Arms, and everything else likely to impede their escape, were thrown away. The Royal forces, seeing their opportunity, took full advantage of it, and, pursuing the enemy, slaughtered about two hundred of them in their flight. The number killed in the town was about one hundred and fifty, while many were wounded.

At Brookhill.

During the succeeding night the news of the battle reached Brookhill, in the Crumlin district, and it was reported that Commodore Watson had fallen. The alarm was immediately given, and early on the following morning every man in the Brookhill yeomanry corps presented himself at the muster in a large field above the family mansion. With them paraded a large number of Orangemen, many of whose descendants tell the story as they heard it from their fathers. Women and children were present to take, as they thought, a last farewell of those most likely, in a few hours, to be engaged in sanguinary conflict. Colonel John Watson, who had seen good service in Flanders under the Duke of York, was on a visit to his brother at the time, and he undertook to lead the corps, observing, as he did so, that he was afraid they should not see the Commodore again. The men, after listening to his address, marched off to Antrim; but, when about half way to that town, they met their own Captain, and greeted him with loud cheers. The Colonel proposed to continue the journey at the head of the corps, while his brother proceeded home; but the Commodore replied, "While I live no one shall lead my men but myself." He then assumed their command, and proceeded to Antrim, where they found the buildings much wrecked, and learned with joy that the Loyalists had won their first and glorious victory over the rebels.

Lord O'Neill.

The fate of Lord O'Neill was deeply mourned. After having been piked on the bridge, his Lordship was removed to Antrim Castle, the seat of the Earl of Massereene, where he received the best medical treatment and the most careful nursing; but mortification of the wounds set in, and he died on the 18th of June, eleven days after the battle. "The atrocious murder of such a man," said the Belfast News-Letter,"and such a landlord in his own country, and so near to his own house, is an addition to the black catalogue of crimes of which United Irishmen have been guilty. From the knowledge that every individual in the country had of him, it was to have been expected that every arm would have been stretched out to defend him in the hour of danger. This melancholy event has proved that with United Irishmen neither gratitude to him who was one of the best of landlords, nor respect for such a character as he possessed, was sufficient protection against assassination." The funeral took place from Shane's Castle at noon on Friday, the 22nd of June, when the remains of a noble and deeply lamented Viscount were deposited in the family vault, convenient to his residence.

As he had been Colonel of the Antrim regiment, as well as Governor of the County, the cortege was marshalled in military order. In front marched the firing party, with arms reversed, followed by the horse he had ridden at Antrim, now led by one of the sergeants of the regiment. Next came the clergy, after them the doctors, and then the hearse containing the body, drawn by six horses. The pall bearers were - The Earl of Massereene, the Honourable C. Skeffington, the Honourable Major Tufton, Captain Gorman, Captain Wakefield, and Captain Rainey. Immediately after the hearse walked the chief mourners, members of the family, followed by the military bands of the 64th and Monaghan Regiments, playing the "Dead March in Saul". Succeeding these were the domestics of the Castle, the principal tenants, the officers of the garrisons of Shane's Castle and Antrim, the Belfast Yeomanry Cavalry, the Magheragall Yeomen Cavalry, a detachment of the 22nd Light Dragoons, the Toome Yeomanry, the gentry of the county, and large numbers of the people. His Lordship was succeeded in his title and estates by his son, Charles Viscount O'Neill, who was not only Governor of the County, but Grand Master of the Orangemen of Antrim.

Fate of M'Cracken.

M'Cracken was defeated, but his personal courage remained. In compliance with his general order, pompously dated, "1st year of Liberty, 6th of June, 1798," Orr's forces drove the garrison of fifty yeomen out of Randalstown, after a stubborn defence of the market

The Execution of Henry Joy McCracken, 17th July 1798

house in which they were quartered, destroyed the greater part of the town, and marched to Toome, from which they fled, when General Knox arrived at the head of a large body of yeomen from the neighbourhood of Dungannon. Having collected his scattered supporters, M'Cracken resolved to advance to Ballymena, then in possession of the rebels, to retrieve the disaster at Antrim. It was not so easy, however, to restore courage to people who had become a disorderly mob. Still, they straggled forward, some halting, disbanding, and returning to their homes, while others accompanied the Generalissimo to Donegore hill.

There M'Cracken soon discovered that he had lost both authority and power. He was surrounded by a Royalist force of four hundred men, commanded by Colonel Clavering, who proposed to the rebels a full and free pardon on delivering up four of their chiefs, for whom he personally offered a reward Of £400, which was refused. It has been said that Clavering conceived it imprudent to attack men whom circumstances had rendered desperate - but their desperation would not have availed much against the opposing force. The truth is - as subsequently told by M'Cleverty, one of the Carrickfergus invalids, who had been on some business at Ballycarry, and was carried as prisoner to the hill - the rebels disagreed among themselves, and, acting on his advice, fifteen hundred of them left the camp, broke and destroyed their arms, and swore they would never again carry an offensive weapon against the King or his loyal subjects. Hundreds of others followed their example; so that in the end, of the 3,200 men on the hill, only fifty remained with M'Cracken. There was nothing for it, therefore, but that he should try to escape. Accordingly, he withdrew with his fifty followers, who soon dwindled down to seven, and, after wandering about for some time - unable to penetrate into Wicklow or Kildare, as he had hoped, or to make his way to the place he had arranged to go on board a ship and quit the country - he was arrested by four Carrickfergus yeomen, and suffered the extreme penalty of the law in Belfast.

Spread of the Trouble.

The action in the town of Antrim was supported by risings in various parts of the country, although they did not occur simultaneously. A large camp of insurgents, computed at ten thousand, was formed at Ballymoney. A detachment of this force, numbering 400, attacked Larne

27

on the morning of the 7th of June, but was gallantly driven off by a subaltern and eighteen men of the Tay Fencibles, aided by yeomanry and loyal inhabitants. In the fight, two privates were killed, while the officer and two privates were wounded. On the 8th of June, another movement at Ballymoney was reported, and, without delay, Lord Henry Murray, Colonel of the 2nd Royal Manx Fencibles, marched from Coleraine on the morning of the 9th, in the hope of meeting the enemy. The troops that accompanied him consisted of part of his own corps, the Dunluce Cavalry, commanded by Captain Macnaghten; and the Dunluce Infantry, commanded by Captain Stuart, the whole column, which had two field pieces, totalling 327 rank and file.

Nothing could have surpassed the ardour of the commander, officers, and men as they marched forth, in defence of King and country, and great was their disappointment, on arriving at the prospective scene of operations, to find that the rebels had moved on to Ballymena. Ballymoney was almost deserted, most of the residents having joined the ranks of treason, and punishment was-meted out accordingly. The majority of the houses, including a few of those inhabited by Loyalists, were burned to the ground, and other property considered likely to be of use to the insurgents was destroyed. Lord Henry sent forward parties to reconnoitre, but, these returning without hearing tidings of any United men, he decided to march back to Coleraine.

Carrickfergus.

Signs of serious trouble manifested themselves at Carrickfergus soon after the start of the revolutionary movement; but Orangemen were there, and they were joined by several young men of the town. All told, the Loyalists numbered about l50, under command of Mr. Henry Nash, County Surveyor, and Mr. Richard Chaplin, of the Excise, and they were on constant duty with the regular troops of the garrison. The proclamation of General Nugent, offering pardon to the disaffected if they returned peaceably to their homes and delivered up their arms within a prescribed time, and threatening that, otherwise, the district would be wasted, had a good effect. It was evident, however, to the rebels that the strength and zeal of the Orangemen, whether as yeomen or volunteers, rendered their cause hopeless. Therefore, arms were surrendered without delay, and further destruction of life and property averted. Indeed, matters had improved to such an extent on the l2th of June that the disturbed parts of the country were announced to have resumed their normal quietness. Having seen their folly, the deluded people repented of it, and Antrim to-day is one of the most thoroughly Orange and loyal parts of the Empire.

Indeed, it may be said, with perfect approach to the truth, that had M'Cracken and other Protestant leaders, given less heed to the seductive arguments addressed to them by conspirators who neither loved them nor Britain, and estimated the French Revolution at its proper value, the rebellion would never have found any support in Ulster. In a few years, descendants of the men who fought and fell, in conflict with the Royal forces, or helped forward the revolutionary movement, were to be found among the best friends of law and order, and, in later times, standing in opposition to Home Rule and Papal tyranny.

COUNTY DOWN.

On the 9th of June, the rebels of County Down first appeared in arms at Saintfield, where they chose Oghley Hill for their camp and base of operations. On the same day another large body of them entered the town of Bangor, where they compelled many to join their ranks. It soon appeared that robbery was the chief motive of these miscreants, one of their first acts being the plunder of Mr. Ward's house. The Rev. James Clewlow, at much personal risk, approached the insurgents, and represented the fatal consequences of their proceedings but his remonstrances were in vain. They repaired to a hill near Newtownards, where a camp was formed, and preparations were made for entering more actively into the struggle. Here, however, quarrels arose, and, in consequence, the Bangor contingent left for home. The arms that had been taken from Mr. Ward's were restored by these insurgents, who next requested Mr. Clewlow to get them protection from General Nugent. That clergyman readily consented to act on their behalf, and set out for Belfast, where General Nugent was; but, before his return, two Presbyterian ministers had, through charges of cowardice and other influences, compelled them to resume their arms, and march to Scrabo. Later they proceeded with their comrades to Saintfield, and plundered a number of houses.

A Fiendish Act.

Immediately after the junction of the rebel forces, one of the most fiendish acts on record was perpetrated. It was, indeed, a human holocaust, and, for cruel and blood-thirsty barbarity exceeded the tragedy at Scullabogue Barn. The reiterated threats of the United Irishmen, which were to confiscate the property of all who refused to join them, caused many to seek protection by being enrolled. Still, a large number of respectable families, chiefly members of the Established Church, sternly declined to secure safety on such humiliating terms, and among them was one distinguished for mildness and moderation, social and domestic virtues. Its members bore the name of M'Kee, and they resided about a mile from Saintfield, near to the road which then led to Belfast. Having always maintained friendly relations with their neighbours, they apprehended no danger, and remained in their home. Twelve months previously, their head, Mr. Hugh M'Kee, a peaceable, industrious citizen, and a genuine Loyalist, had occasion to prosecute several United Irishmen for an attack upon his house, which was a substantial two-storey building; but it was never thought by him that there would be any repetition of such trouble. At the time, then, of this dreadful occurrence in 1798, he and his wife, with seven sons and two daughters, besides a maidservant, were reposing in confident security, never having had a personal quarrel with anyone.

It was stated in the rebel camp, however, that this innocent man entertained some designs against the United Irishmen, and strangers believed the story which those who knew him well indignantly repudiated. A party was, therefore, formed to punish the alleged offender, and make an onslaught on his home. After partaking freely of whisky, and rousing their fury, they proceeded to their savage work, armed with guns, pistols, pikes, pitchforks, and other rude weapons. It was the night of the 9th of June when they set out on their terrible errand, and they moved stealthily along in the darkness, no one suspecting their presence.

The building, constructed with no windows at the rear, while an open space was in front, formed a rather serious obstacle to their immediate success, especially when the inmates were in an attitude of defence, and it so happened that this difficulty had to be met. Alarmed by the noise, and fearing violence, Mr. M'Kee and his family prepared to protect themselves. The rebels then sent to the camp for reinforcements, and, when these had come up, renewed the attack by firing into the house, the inmates offering a gallant resistance. For some time the unequal struggle went on, the assailants receiving severe punishment, until, despairing of carrying out their murderous intentions in a more cruel form, they fired the building. All further attempts at defence were now futile, and Mr. M'Kee and the others with him endeavoured to escape from the burning dwelling; but the moment any of them came to the window, they were received by deadly volleys. Mrs. M'Kee was the first to make an effort to leave, and it might be thought that, having regard to the honour paid to her sex, her life would have been spared. She had, however, no sooner appeared at the door than she was riddled with bullets, and her inanimate body fell back into the flames. The servant man, who was a Roman Catholic, next presented himself at an upper window, from which the party in the rear could hear his voice. He called for mercy as a "Catholic and a brother", and, upon the strength of this plea, ventured out of the house, letting himself down from the window; but, on touching the ground, he was met by a general discharge of musketry. Although badly wounded, he did not fall until some of the barbarians pursued and most inhumanely piked him. He was left for dead, but, after being found, he lived for twenty-four hours, and told the tragic fate of his master and family.

The innocent people, seeing that they could not effect their escape, determined to die together, and collected in a group at one end of the house. In this way they met their end in a terrible form, the rebels rejoicing at the conflagration, and hearing unmoved the lamentable and piercing cries of father and children, and maidservant.

It is no wonder that the blood of Loyalists begins to boil when they think of such terrible deeds as this perpetrated in the dead of night. Yet a number of writers, both present and past, have tried to make the world believe that the blood-thirsty wretches who committed murder and rapine on unoffending citizens, were a host of fair-faced angels, who covered themselves and their country with glory. Shame on such sentiment ! It is too fulsome and satanic to be entertained by any but members of an assassination society, what the majority of the United Irishmen were. Far better would it be for these vaunters in print to let the deeds of their heroes rot with their bones, than, by flattering tributes, draw aside the curtain of forgetfulness and expose their memory, in the light of honest historical investigation, to the well-merited sentence of eternal infamy.

As to the horror of this June night, it remains to be said that twelve persons were arrested, and brought to trial before Lord Kilwarden at the next Downpatrick Spring Assizes. An alibi was set up for each of the accused; but they were all found guilty. Three were executed on the Saturday following the conviction; seven were ordered to be executed on Saturday, the 6th of April; and two were respited until May.

One need not wonder that there were yeomanry excesses on the other side. The flames in which this family perished were still smouldering over charred remains when other flames were kindled in Saintfield, and the excited Loyalists gave victory a burnt offering.

As soon as the news reached Belfast that the insurgents had assembled at Scrabo Hill, General Nugent ordered the 22nd Light Dragoons, the Monaghan Militia, the Fifeshire Fencibles, and the yeomanry cavalry and infantry corps, with two guns, and a detachment of the Royal Irish Artillery, commanded by Major-General Barber, to disperse the camp; but on their arrival at the place not a rebel was to be seen.

Fight at Saintfield.

Colonel Stapleton, who commanded at Newtownards, when informed that the United men had gathered at Saintfield, marched to the latter town on Sunday, the 10th of June. The force under him consisted of a detachment of the York Fencibles, also the Newtownards and Comber yeomen, cavalry, and infantry, who totalled altogether about 320 men, with two fieldpieces. Teeling says that "before any formidable number" of the insurgents had assembled, they were forced into action; but a more impartial version of the narrative gives their number at 6,000 or 7,000,* and states that they fought desperately. Hearing of the advance of the Royalists, the rebels formed an ambuscade at a hollow part of the road, on either side of which were high, close hedges, in full leaf, affording them complete concealment.

 The place they had chosen for this purpose was about a quarter of a mile from Saintfield, and Stapleton's column had to pass through it. The body in ambush numbered 3,000 men, while the remainder occupied Oghley Hill on the right. Unconscious of the dangerous proximity of the enemy, the Royalists continued their march. About the time that Stapleton and his small army were approaching the ambuscade, they were joined by the Rev. Mr. Mortimer, Vicar of Portaferry, and his nephew, and seven or eight yeomen from that town.

32   * Belfast News-Letter, June 12, 1798

This clergyman, always conspicuous for his loyalty, was soon after recognized by one of the insurgents, who, taking deliberate aim, shot him dead. Had it not been for the rashness of the concealed murderers, Colonel Stapleton's column might have been surrounded and cut off, for it had got into the defile, where the road was too narrow for the troops to deploy. A bloody engagement began immediately. Those of the Royalists who attempted to cross into the fields to form were shot down, or butchered with pikes. Stapleton's courage, however, was equal to the occasion. Forcing his way through a hedge he got the grenadier company into a field, and opened his guns with such effect that the fortune of the day was changed. The action now became general. The troops who had not entered the defile were able to manoeuvre, and though for a time vigorously assailed by the rebels, the Royalists eventually gained the victory, and compelled the enemy to retreat to Newtownards, while Stapleton marched his men to Comber, and proceeded next day to Belfast.

The United men, by their own account, lost upwards of 500 killed, among whom were several leaders dressed in green jackets, turned up with white or yellow, white vests, buckskin smallclothes, half-boots, hats trimmed with white cock-neck feathers and green cockades. The total loss of the Royalists was twenty-nine killed, twenty-two wounded, and three missing. Besides the loyal Vicar of Portaferry, Captain Chetwynd, Lieutenant White, and Ensign James Sparkes were killed. Lieutenant Edenson was wounded. Brave Chetwynd, who fought valiantly at the head of his company, received nine pike wounds, but still kept his position, encouraging his men. At length two musket bullet wounds deprived him of life, and the country of his services. Lieutenant White also fell gallantly at the head of his men. "Poor Sparkes," says the Belfast News-Letter of that time, "whose race of glory was now completed, was only sixteen years of age; and had, just before he fell, received for his courageous conduct the public approbation of his commanding officer." From the same source we learn that "too much praise cannot be given to the Newtownards and Comber yeomen cavalry and infantry, who, commanded by Captains Rose-Clelland and Houghton, showed great intrepidity during the whole of the action."

Newtownards and Donaghadee.

On the day following the fight at Saintfield, the rebels attacked a few invalids who were in charge of stores in Newtownards market-house, and forced them to capitulate. A large body of them also entered Donaghadee, broke open, and plundered the shops. Fortunately the officials of the Revenue and Post Office, with the official papers, and nearly all the Loyalists, had got on board one of the packets the evening previous, their embarkation being covered by a cutter which Lord Ranelagh had ordered thither. The rebels indulged freely in whisky and wine they had stolen, and continued in a state of riot and intoxication for three days; but, at length, they succumbed to a woman's stratagem. Among the Protestants who remained in their houses was a lady named Hamilton, who, tired of having the town in the hands of a drunken mob, ascended to the attic of her dwelling, put her head out of the skylight, and shouted at the top of her voice, "The dragoons are coming !" The alarm was false, but it produced the intended effect. Immediately the rebels threw down their arms and fled, leaving potions unfinished, and the prisoners, whom they had captured, unharmed.

Portaferry.

In the afternoon of the 10th, a United force, one thousand strong, attacked the town of Portaferry, whose small garrison consisted of the local yeomanry corps, under Captain Charles Mathews, and a few Orange Volunteers. Although this has been classed among minor engagements in Down, it had an important bearing on the general issue. The plan of the insurgents, which showed some head, was, after taking the town, to cross the ferry, proceed, with whatever they could obtain in Lecale, and attack Downpatrick, presuming that the troops in garrison would either march as they had done, to co-operate with General Nugent at Ballynahinch, or remain to meet the assault.

In the latter case, Nugent would be deprived of valuable assistance, and, in the former, the town would be exposed to the insurgents. The brave little garrison, however, disarranged the programme. Fortunately Captain Mathews got information in the morning concerning the intended attack. The yeomanry were, accordingly, posted in the market-house, the arches of which they filled with a dry temporary wall to prevent the enemy setting fire to the loft; while the Orange Volunteers did duty outside the building. Teeling, who tries to rob the yeomen of the praise that impartial history has awarded them, admits that Captain Mathews was a brave and experienced veteran, and displayed considerable talent in defence of the town; but General Nugent did justice to both Captain and men. Immediately the pikemen appeared in the open street, a volley was fired from the market-house, accompanied by shots from the two swivel guns outside, worked by the Orange Volunteers, and a number of the enemy fell. The United men advanced a second time, and another volley from the yeomen and their Orange comrades sent death again into the rebel ranks. Then the guns of the revenue cruiser in the river, commanded by Captain Hopkins, began to tell with effect, and, in a short time, the insurgents retreated in disorder, leaving behind them about forty dead, while many more were carried away. On the Royal side not a yeoman was hurt; but three of the Orange Volunteers, who served the swivels, having no cover, were killed. The rebels were said to have been under the command of a Presbyterian probationer, subsequently executed. At any rate, their captains were a shopkeeper in Portaferry and two farmers in its vicinity.

Ballynahinch.

The Northern insurgents made their great fight at Ballynahinch. This town stands on the Annacloy or Ballynahinch river, and occupies the centre of an attractive and prosperous district. The manor was granted by Charles the Second to Sir George Rawdon, ancestor of the Marquis of Hastings. A family of ancient origin, the name being derived from the parish of Rawdon, in Yorkshire, its members were held in good repute as landlords in the County Down. Lord Moira, who began his great improvements at Montalto in 1770, was a colonel of the Union Regiment of Volunteers, and objected to become a member of the Northern Whig Club, observing that, although anxious to abolish acknowledged abuses, he had no wish for revolution. He seceded from the Volunteers, with Lord Charlemont, on the question of extending to Roman Catholics plenary enfranchisement and power in the State. At his Lordship's death, on the 20th of June, 1793, he had spent £30,000 in improving the town and estate, which passed into the hands of Mr. David Ker, of Portavo, and still remains in that family.

On the 11th of June, before the conflict, which occurred on the 12th and 13th of June, 1798, the rebels collected 7,000 strong at Saintfield, and, finding themselves without a leader, owing to the arrest of Dickson, they unanimously elected Henry Munro, of Lisburn, as Generalissimo. Munro was a man of much spirit and enterprise, but it would have been well for his family, and those whom he led, or misled, if he had

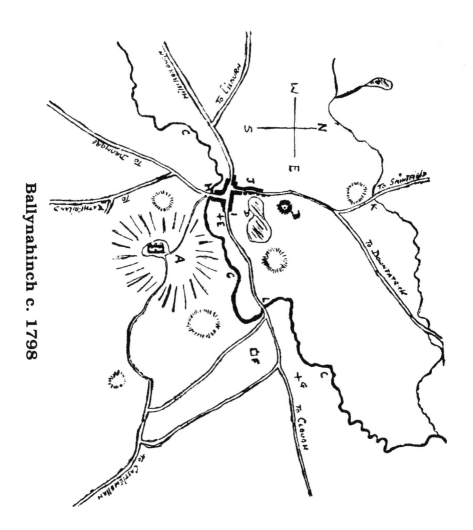

Ballynahinch c. 1798

attended to his calling as a linen merchant, and let playing at soldiers alone. Notwithstanding all that has been said of his romantic and chivalrous nature, his vigour and activity, and ardent love of glory, he was evidently not qualified to discharge the duties of a general officer in the field. Instantly he was invested with power, he despatched a force under command of Townshend, to take possession of Ballynahinch, a very few of whose inhabitants sympathized with the insurgents, who were said to have "come from the eastern part of the county, just as the plague of locusts had come from the east into Egypt". The population of the town totalled about 800, and most of this number had sought safety in Lisburn and other parts of the country. Townshend formed a camp on the lawn in front of Lord Moira's castle, while Munro's forces remained at Creevy Rocks, a high and rugged hill about one mile from Saintfield.

Camp at Creevy Rocks.

A writer in the Belfast Magazine, a Presbyterian minister, has left on record the following description of Munro's camp, and the proceedings connected with it:

"Here were assembled a motley crowd of men and boys, women and children. From this rendezvous orderlies were despatched to summon the county to turn out in arms. I was privileged with a sight of two of these messengers. One of them on horseback, clad in green, traversed the neighbourhood, and, with sword in hand, commanded the youth, in the name of the nation, to turn out and fight for their country's rights. Another on foot, or rather in disguise, as if impressed with fear, or conscious of guilt; privately whispered his errand to such as he thought he might venture to trust. The battle to which this poor fellow warned others was fatal to himself; for he was blown to pieces by a cannon ball. The camp ground was loaded with prisoners, partly brought to the place by friends of the cause, and partly taken, without leave or pay, as the right of warriors. Many visited the camp from curiosity, who had no intention of fighting, and who never thought of the evil of appearing under arms in open rebellion. Many who were armed were undisciplined, and knew nothing of the difficulty, nor reflected on the danger of meeting a regular force on the field of conflict. Some were clothed with offices to which they had been elected, and others assumed command; some were disposed to obey orders, others were not. A bold and enterprising individual, but rude in tactics, arrogating the rank of officer, and mustering a number from a disorderly crowd, gave the order 'Dress.' 'D—— you,' said an impudent novice, 'I'll run my pike through your body if you command me to dress.' On the forenoon of one of the days of encampment, a few yeomen cavalry from Hillsborough appeared on a distant eminence, surveying the camp. At first sight, they produced a little consternation; but on being observed not to be numerous, they were often saluted with a loud and long huzza, especially on retiring from the place of reconnoitre. Reports, wild as imagination could conceive in her highest flights, and false as fame had ever circulated, were wafted by hundreds, as if on the wings of the wind, from the country to the camp, and from the camp to the country, chiefly relating to the numbers on both sides."

The Military.

All eyes were now turned to Ballynahinch, in which town a party of soldiers arrived on the morning of Sunday. They came exactly in time, says the writer just quoted, to rescue two or three yeomen, whom some of the more hardy insurgents had caught, and were just about to hang. Encouraged by the non-arrival of the military on Saturday, the safety of the night, and the return of a fine day,-the rebels were boldly proceeding, without trial or ceremony, to despatch a few of the reputed enemy. These devoted victims escaped an awful death. Those who had seized, judged, and were about to execute them fled; but in the following week one of them, a lad of seventeen, was hung at Newry by order of a court-martial. The soldiers who arrived at Ballynahinch had been at the Battle of Antrim, and, having regard to what had occurred at Saintfield, their orders were to await the arrival of a larger force, the intention being to attack the camp at Creevy Rocks, which was flushed with success, and stimulated- by the report that at Saintfield the United men had routed the Royal army. The state of feeling in the neighbourhood is sketched as follows:

"The country was all in motion. Some hesitated what side to join. Some determined to join neither; but were much perplexed in devising means of safety from the soldiers and from the people. Goods and furniture were carried to places of concealment and of supposed safety. Many had passed a sleepless night, not a little perplexed with real or imaginary dangers. Some left the neighbourhood, and, the better to cover their departure from a scene of disturbance, and to escape in safety, summoned the people, as they themselves retreated from the theatre of action, to turn out and repair to the camp.... At the houses some were very busy sharpening their pikes and preparing for action; others, armed with these weapons, were proceeding to the camp."

Rebels March to Ballynahinch.

On Monday, the 11th of June, Munro and the main body of his forces marched to Ballynahinch; and, having joined Townshend, he placed some of his best musketeers in ambush at the base of Windmill Hill, which the Royal forces had to pass. The command of this division was given to an officer named M'Cance, while the Generalissimo took post on Edenavady Hill. This place, which was of considerable height, lay nearly half a mile south-west of Ballynahinch, and it appeared well fitted for the purpose of the rebels. The portion next the town was occupied. It presented an open space on all sides, beyond which the country was studded with clumps of trees.

Upon their arrival, the insurgents despatched parties in all directions, for the double object of collecting provisions and bringing in the United Irishmen. The men, however, were not in haste to get to the camp, choosing rather to retire to Slieve Croob and the other adjoining mountains. With respect to foraging there was more success, the heaviest threats being employed against those who delayed sending provisions to the army of the Union. The fighting men were on the mountains; the old men, females, and boys were at their houses; and some from fear, others from love, set to work to prepare oaten cakes and boil large quantities of salted beef and bacon for the forces on Edenavady.

Camp at Edenavady.

The camp is described as follows by a person who, with his sisters, visited it, bringing in provisions: "When we arrived, there were on the ground a considerable number of females, chiefly servants, or the daughters, or wives, of cotters or small farmers. These were almost all employed on the same business as ourselves; though, it is said, that two or three of them remained on the field during the battle, submitting to their share of its labours and dangers, and performing as valiant deeds as the men. Nothing could surpass the delicacy and kindness with which these female visitors were received and conducted through the camp.... Everything was explained with minuteness; pikes of different constructions were pointed out, and their uses explained; the cannon and the ammunition were shown, and the tremendous effects glanced at which they were calculated to produce.

The leaders were also pointed out - the more distinguished and the greater favourites among them - with pride and exultation; and their dresses were also explained. To me, as well as to my companions, the whole was a series of wonders; everything was striking, and even imposing and delightful. The eye was presented with a mixed and motley multitude; some walking about; others stretched listlessly on the green turf, along the field; a considerable number sheltering themselves from the scorching rays of a burning sun, under the shade of the trees, with which the field was skirted; and many restoring nature with the sweets of balmy sleep. They wore no uniforms, yet they presented a tolerably decent appearance, being dressed, no doubt, in their Sunday's clothes - some better and some worse; but none in the ragged costume that is often to be seen in other parts of Ireland.

The only thing in which they all concurred was the wearing of green, almost every individual having a knot of ribbons of that colour, sometimes intermixed with yellow, in his hat. Most of them, besides, had their hats and buttonholes decorated with laurel from the adjoining grounds. Their leaders, also, in general, wore green or yellow belts, and some of them green coats. Many wore both of them, while those under their command bore ornaments of various descriptions, and of different degrees of taste and execution, the most of which had been presented as tributes of regard and affection, and as incentives to heroic deeds, by females, whose breasts beat as high in patriotic ardour as those of their husbands, their sweethearts, or their brothers. The most common of these decorations were the harp entwined with shamrock or bays, but without the crown; the British lion and unicorn in a falling attitude; the cap of liberty; and many other symbolic representations, with various corresponding inscriptions, expressive of the wishes and feelings of the people, such as 'Liberty or Death', 'A Downfall to Tyrants', and 'Freedom in Ireland', and many others of a similar character. In their arms there was as great a diversity as in their dress. By far the majority had pikes, which were truly formidable instruments in close fight, but of no use in distant warfare. These had generally wooden shafts, seven or eight feet long, with sharpened heads of steel, of different forms, and commonly ten or twelve inches in length. Some of these heads consisted simply of one longitudinal piece; but others had another piece crossing this, and forming a sort of hook, which was thought likely to be of use in dragging horsemen from their seats, or in cutting the bridles of their horses. A number had old swords, generally of the least efficient kind; and some had merely pitch-forks.

Those of the higher class were armed with guns. There were also seven or eight pieces of cannon, mounted on common cars, which were not calculated to produce much effect. The army was composed chiefly of persons in youth and middle life; with not a few, however, on the precincts of old age; or on the borders between boyhood and youth. All seemed to carry a cheerful expression of countenance; but which from subsequent appearance, I would consider, in most cases, to have been affected; and I have no doubt but a more skilful observer would have detected traits of doubt, and even of fear, in a great many faces which seemed lighted up with gaiety and smiles."

Munro's Proclamation.

This description, new to many, bears the stamp of truth, and forms a striking contrast to the fanciful sketches of Teeling, who had not the advantage of personal observation. The people were intoxicated with excitement, and most of them were in the camp, because they had been previously sworn in as members of the conspiracy. There is evidence, however, of lukewarmness in the cause having already begun. The reinforcements expected were not coming in, and the commissariat was poorly supplied to maintain 7,000 or 17,000, both numbers being given as the strength of the army of boys and girls, and persons of middle life, rudely armed and ill-adapted to meet the Royal forces. Munro's feeling can be read in the proclamation he issued, and the letter he addressed at the same time to Townshend, then in command of the division occupying the town of Ballynahinch. The proclamation, which was displayed in the original, ran as follows:

"General Munro's Proclamation. To his Army and the Inhabitants of the County Down. Not to pay any Rent to disaffected Landlords, as such Rent is confiscated to the use of the National Liberty War. Head Quarters, Ballynahinch, l2th June, l798."

The letter to Townshend indicated more fully the difficulties in the way of the Generalissimo. Copies of both documents were produced at the court-martial in Lisburn, and admitted by the author to be his handwriting. To Townshend he wrote:

"Worthy Citizen - We have had some small reinforcements say 300 men. I hear yours is much more. I hope the Defenders have rallied to you. Send me express. I send you some ban cartridges. You must press for provisions as we do. I will send you some more to-day, and anything that can be got here."

"Tuesday Morning."   "Munro."
"The Citizens are all in choice spirits, longing for action. Health and Respect."

As the eye-witness says, they "seemed to carry a cheerful expression of countenance." The leaders kept moving through the field, speaking familiarly and kindly to the men, cheering their courage, making jokes to suit their tastes, and exciting laughter among the groups of the army of the Union; but the jokes and the resultant mirth were destined to be of short duration.

Nugent's Advance.

On the morning of Tuesday, the 12th of June, two divisions of the Royal troops and their auxiliaries moved from different points; and, according to preconcerted arrangements, were to meet at the junction of two roads, a short distance from Ballynahinch. General Nugent, whose route was from Belfast, via Saintfield, commanded 700 infantry, 150 cavalry, and five pieces of ordnance. This force consisted of a detachment of the 22nd Light Dragoons; the Monaghan regiment, commanded by Colonel Leslie; the Belfast cavalry, at the head of which was Captain Rainey; some yeomen infantry, and a considerable number of Belfast Orangemen, and their brethren of other districts.

As the Royalists proceeded, they were reinforced by the Magheragall cavalry, under the command of Captain Wakefield, who, in the heat of the engagement, along with Commodore Watson, gave distinguished proofs of his ability and courage. Some members of the Magheragall corps, though suffering from wounds received at Antrim, positively refused to remain at home. Before leaving, General Nugent issued a proclamation in the following terms, dated, "Headquarters, Belfast,

June 11, 1798, 5 p.m.":

"Major-General Nugent, commanding his Majesty's forces in the North of Ireland, being desirous of sparing the effusion of human blood, and the total devastation of the County Down, is pleased to, and does hereby extend to the Insurgents in the said county, the same terms of submission and atonement that have been so eagerly and gratefully accepted by many of their equally deluded neighbours in the County of Antrim, to wit:

"That if those unfortunate persons, who, by the arts of selfish and designing people, have been seduced from their allegiance to the true and lawful Sovereign, his Majesty King George the Third, to become rebels and traitors to their country} will return to their duty as faithful and peaceable subjects, and to their respective houses and occupations, the General positively and surely engages to them that no one whatever in the county (with the exception hereafter mentioned) shall be molested or their property injured; and that, as a proof of their return to loyalty and good government, they must in the course of twenty-four hours after the date of this proclamation (making allowance for the more distant parts of the county) liberate all the persons of every description now in their custody, and send them to their respective places of abode; and that they also depute some persons to receive all their arms and offensive weapons of every denomination, with the ammunition belonging thereto, who shall be sent to the General to know where they are to be deposited; and that they also deliver up the principal persons who have been most active in instigating, or compelling them to engage in their late wicked practices.

"Should the above injunctions not be complied with within the time specified, Major-General Nugent will proceed to set fire to and totally destroy the towns of Killinchy, Killyleagh Ballynahinch, Saintfield, and every cottage and farmhouse in the vicinity of these places, carry off the stock and cattle, and put everyone to the sword who may be found in arms.

"It particularly behoves all the well-affected persons, who are now with the rebels from constraint, arid who, it is known, form a considerable part of their numbers, to exert themselves in having these terms complied with, as it is the only opportunity there will be of rescuing themselves and properties from the indiscriminate vengeance of an army, necessarily let loose upon them."

The Country Devastated.

The terms of the Proclamation were not complied with and Nugent kept his word. Saintfield was already in ashes, and from Saintfield to Ballynahinch the progress of the Royal forces was announced by the smoke and flames of farmhouses fired indiscriminately. It was nothing new in warfare; and they grievously malign the Orange yeomen and Orange volunteers, who attribute the devastation to them. In this case the alarming conditions of the country imposed serious responsibility upon General Nugent. Those, therefore, who lived at the time and were best qualified to form an opinion, attributed the commanding officer's severity to a desire to terrify the insurgents, secure the release of the people whom they had coerced into the camp, and prevent the shedding of blood.

If such were the objects of the harshly-worded Proclamation, they signally failed; for, instead of being soothed, the rebels were exasperated, and many who were not rebels shared their feeling. On perceiving the flames, all those who had remained in their dwellings made haste to remove such articles as were regarded most valuable, and could b easily concealed. Beds and wearing apparel, barrels of meal, flitches of beef and bacon, and casks of butter were deposited in meadows and cornfields, in the bottoms of ditches, in gardens, and rubbish, or in whatever other places were considered least likely to attract suspicion. In one instance, and, no doubt, in many more not recorded, the lease of a arm, with other papers and some money, was deposited under a large stone in the middle of a field. In another case, in the same neighbourhood, one hundred guineas were placed in a magpie's nest on a tall tree. The household goods and leases and cash having been disposed of, their owners fled to the mountains, abandoning the houses to their fate.

The March from Downpatrick.

The second division of the Royal forces marched from Downpatrick, under command of Lieutenant-Colonel Stewart, who had with him part of his own regiment, the 33rd, a strong detachment of the Argyle Fencibles, thirty cavalry, the Downpatrick, Castlewellan, and other yeomanry corps, also a contingent of Orangemen. The Downpatrick corps was commanded by Captain Maxwell, and numbered one hundred men, nearly all Orangemen. Two of hem were the brothers

Matthew and William Skyline, members of Lodge No. 430, established in the parish of Inch. William fell at Ballynahinch, and was the only yeoman killed. He had been initiated in the year 1797, and his name is seventh on the list of the original members of the lodge.

According to the arrangements previously agreed to, the two divisions net at the junction of the roads, directly opposite the rebel camp The number of the combined forces was now about 1,500 of all ranks; and they were to oppose from 7,000 to 10,000, some put the figures higher, occupying advantageous positions, and lying in entrenchments. From first to last, however, it was well known that numbers would not compensate for defective tactics, and imperfect discipline. If Munro and his staff had known their business, the Downpatrick division of Royalists might have been demolished. It was comparatively weak, and its arrival was so ill-timed that two hours elapsed before Nugent's column appeared. But Munro's knowledge of military affairs was limited to what he had learned in a volunteer corps, and he was surrounded by colonels and captains more ignorant than himself. Hence, one splendid opportunity for the rebels was lost, and they did lot get another chance.

The Battle.

The approach of Nugent and his column was reported to Munro, who despatched 500 men, under the command of a leader named Johnston, to occupy an eminence adjoining the ambuscade at Windmill Hill, entrusted to M'Cance. The movement was ill-judged, and attended with failure. A hot battle now became inevitable, having regard to the positions of the opposing forces. Nugent, in supreme command of the Royal forces, which were between the hill and the town, opened fire on both places. This was about six o'clock in the evening, and the battle, in which musketry and cannon played an important part raged until about nine, when darkness put an end to hostilities. During the three hours' combat the advantages were on the side of the Royalists. Already Ballynahinch was partially in flames, and Townshend had no choice but to retreat. The Windmill Hill was cleared by the fire of the guns and the majority of those who had been sent to reinforce M'Cance deserted. An "Eye-witness" says -

> "Soon after the commencement of the engagement many began to slink away from the field, and we distinctly heard their more determined fellows shouting to stop the runaways. The chief

desertion, however, took place in the dusk of the evening and during the night, when the darkness afforded the cowardly an opportunity of stealing away unperceived, and the interruption of the conflict gave them time to cool and reflect on the horrors of the fight.... One of the fugitives who passed our station the following morning was in such confusion that, though it was only two hours after sunrise, he thought it was near sunset; and, looking towards the horizon, thanked God in the most devout manner.... as he would have a better chance of escaping. A similar state of mind was shown by many others."

At the close of the day, victory rested with Nugent, who ascended the hill, where, after hanging a rebel colonel named M'Cullough, the Royal troops encamped for the night, and prepared to make a final attack next morning. A heavy volley poured upon the military by insurgent musketeers, who had worked their way unobserved to a favourable position, was the only incident worthy of note after the cessation of hostilities. The combatants remained quiet throughout the night, nothing being heard save an occasional shout, or the firing of a sentinel's gun.

Some have blamed Munro for having failed to profit by the advice of impetuous subordinates, who were anxious to attack the Royalists under cover of the darkness, more especially as it is represented that drunkenness prevailed among the troops in the town. But this is neither fair to the rebel commander nor to his opponents. The yeomanry and other loyal forces were too intent upon stamping out the rising to indulge in licentiousness or fall into laxity of discipline at such a crisis, and Munro was well aware of this.

Still, allowing that there were excesses in the town, no one has ventured to make such a charge against Nugent's men on Windmill Hill, and an attack upon their comrades would not have contributed very materially towards ending the contest in favour of the United men. The refusal of Munro, if he was ever approached on the subject at all, cannot, therefore, be said to have contributed towards his defeat on the following day, nor can it be made to explain the desertion of 2,000 Roman Catholics in the dead of night. Musgrave says these fugitives remained about two miles from the scene of strife, on the Seaforde Road, elated to think the Protestants were destroying each other.

Fighting Renewed.

Hostilities were resumed between two and three o'clock on the morning of Wednesday, the 13th of June. General Nugent sent Colonel Stewart, with detachments of the 22nd Light Dragoons and the Argyle Fencibles, and some yeomanry, to take post so as to enfilade the enemy's line. They got possession of a small hill, and, by this manoeuvre, the Royal forces were on the right and left of Ballynahinch, leaving the rebels no choice but to retreat to the mountains. At the same time, Colonel Leslie, and the Monaghan regiment, some regular cavalry, the Magheragall cavalry, yeomen infantry, and Orange Volunteers from Belfast, all under command of Major General Barber, were to march into the town and attack the insurgents there. Two howitzers and six 6-pounders covered the advance of Barber's column, and sent occasional shots to the enemy.

The first act on the part of the Royal forces was to set fire to a number of buildings. Soon after the flames had begun to develop and spread to other houses, the combat became general, Munro replying to the attack with eight pieces of ship cannon. His forces were formed in two divisions, one of which was to penetrate Ballynahinch on the right, while the other, commanded by himself in person, directed its march to the left. Barber's column was furiously attacked by a body of pikemen, who rushed on to the road from Lord Moira's demesne, and charged to the mouth of the guns, one of which they attempted to capture. For a moment the Royal troops wavered, but they immediately rallied, fell upon the assailants vigorously, and repulsed them with heavy loss. Stewart's division also was violently attacked, but the fire from his howitzers and sixpounders proved so galling that the insurgents retreated in disorder.

Meanwhile, Barber and Leslie had penetrated into the centre of the town, where Munro and his forces had already arrived, and a fierce combat ensued. Those of the 22nd Light Dragoons who had survived the battle at Antrim became infuriated, and cut and hacked the rebels without mercy. The same feeling pervaded the Magheragall cavalry, and they, too, displayed great courage. Captain Wakefield's horse, unaccustomed to the roar of cannon, became completely unmanageable, and rushed wildly about, exposing its gallant owner to the fire of friends and foes. At this moment a desperate conflict occurred between the rebels and the Monaghan regiment, supported by yeomen and Orange Volunteers. A number of the former reached the guns of the battalion, but they were soon compelled to retire.

An Eye-witness's Account.

According to "An Eye-witness", "the scene about sunrise was at once terrific and sublime. The smoke and flames which arose from the burning village- the incessant discharges of small arms; the large and frequent flashes of the cannon, and their loud reports, each of which was reverberated with numerous re-echoes from the neighbouring heights, loud and confused, as if the mountains were tumbling down all around; with the occasional bursting of a bomb-shell in the air before it reached the intended distance, all conspired in presenting a scene new to the onlookers, and to most of the combatants themselves, and one that was calculated to impress with awe the stoutest hearts."

The most terrific part of the conflict took place in the streets, and especially in the market square, of Ballynahinch, the rebels there offering most determined resistance to the division commanded by Colonel Leslie. Above the din of battle could be heard the cheers, the yells, and the shrieks of the combatants.

Thus the struggle continued till about seven o'clock, the rebels being literally mown down by the artillery and a cross-fire of musketry. Gradually they became weakened and dispirited by death and desertion, while their fire slackened and almost ceased. Eventually, after four hours' severe fighting, they retreated in disorder. The woods and the nature of the ground hindered the cavalry from long, and effectual pursuit. The troops now passed through the town, and proceeded to clear the field of the few insurgents who had still the courage to await their approach. The Battle of Ballynahinch, which lasted three hours on Tuesday evening and four hours on Wednesday morning, terminated in decisive victory for the loyal forces. The enemies of the Constitution were dispersed, and the disaffected were warned for all time against

> " Those acts of hateful strife! hateful to all,
> Tho' heaviest, by just measure, on themselves
> and their adherents."

The Losses.

The losses have been variously estimated. It would appear however, that more than five hundred rebels were killed on the field and in the flight, and the number wounded must have been proportionately great. The Royal troops were more fortunate for they had only a total of thirty in killed and wounded. Among the former were Captain Evatt and five privates of the Monaghan regiment. Evatt fell early in the morning. He was leading a detachment through the demesne, to dislodge the rebels on the hill when a party of them took post behind a hedge, and fired a volley which cut short the career of a gallant young officer and compelled his men to retire.

Lieutenant Ellis and sixteen men of the Monaghan regiment were wounded The Argyle Fencibles had one man killed and another wounded. Of the yeomen, the only man killed was the one already mentioned; several were slightly wounded. The Royalists captured— some say two and others four—green colours, a green jacket which had been worn by one of the leaders, who was killed, eight one-pounder guns, and three barrels of gunpowder. The guns were not mounted, but they had been frequently fired. Immediately after the battle the troops set out for Belfast, and arrived there in the evening. Besides the trophies named, they carried along with them spoils of various kinds, including many horses taken from the vanquished insurgents. Two of the few prisoners captured were in the hands of the Belfast cavalry.

Nugent's Report.

General Nugent, in his official report to Dublin Castle, stated that both officers and men deserved praise for their zeal and alacrity on this as on all other occasions. He made special and favourable mention of Major-General Barber's services; of the benefit he had derived from the advice and assistance of Lieutenant-Colonel Stewart; of Colonel Leslie's readiness to volunteer for duty at all times ,and of the yeomanry, who had "behaved with extreme steadiness and bravery". General Nugent also named as; entitled to his thanks, Captain Stewart, of the Glenarm Yeomanry; and Captain Mathews, of the Portaferry Yeomanry, who "behaved uncommonly well in repulsing large bodies of rebels, that had attacked them with great fury". Captain Boyd, of the Ballycastle Yeomen, secured a warm encomium from the General.

Having been warned of impending peril Boyd retreated to Coleraine, where he collected the Dunseverick and Giant's Causeway corps, and, at the head of three corps, returned to Ballycastle, and beat the rebels out of the town.

Fate of Munro.

After the fight, Harry Munro, who had tried to rally the few remaining with him on Edenavady Hill, found that further effort was hopeless, and fled at the head of about one hundred and fifty men. These soon followed the example of the others, and on the earliest opportunity left him to look after his own safety. Alone now, he took to the mountains and wandered about, a forlorn and disconsolate figure. Two days after the battle, he was accidentally discovered by three Orangemen, as he lay concealed under some litter in a potato furrow, about six miles from Ballynahinch. "He offered" according to Musgrave, "forty guineas if they would let him escape; but the loyalty of his captors was not to be corrupted." They conveyed him to Hillsborough, along with a young man named Kane, who, taken in the same furrow, was formerly a clerk in the office of the *Northern Star, Belfast, and then, on* the 16th of June, they sent him under guard to Lisburn. Here a trial by court-martial took place on the 18th, and, being found guilty of treason and sentenced, Munro was executed at his own door. His head was afterwards put on a pike, and placed in the market-house. It is said by some writers - and Maxwell is one of them - that his wife and mother witnessed his execution, but the statement is cruel and untrue.

Through the influence of the Rev Dr Cupples, rector of the parish, they were allowed to have an interview with him on the previous day, which was Sunday, and after this they withdrew from the scene. It was owing to the failure of another person to come forward that the leadership had devolved upon poor Munro. The choice was made by lot in Attorney M'Guigan's office in Fountain Lane, Belfast, and he was too much of a man to decline the task, dangerous though it was. As soon as his wife understood the position into which he had been forced, she hastened to her father's at Dunmurry. In the forenoon of the fatal day his mother learned what had happened to her only son, and, closing her little shop in Bow Lane, she remained in seclusion and mourning for several days. After decapitation, Harry's body was interred in a corner of the western section of the burying-ground attached to Lisburn Cathedral, and the spot still attracts the interest of many visiting the town.

A Narrow Escape.

On Munro's case being disposed of, the Rev. Thomas Ledlie Birch was arraigned before the same court-martial on the charge of having encouraged the rebels at Creevy Rocks, on the 10th of June; at Saintfield and Ballynahinch on the 11th of June; and at Mr. Price's Castle on the 12th of June. This prisoner made a defence in which he admitted being present on some of the occasions referred to, but alleged it was in the interests of humanity. After professing love for the King, he assured the court that he would ever pray for his Majesty, and expressed the desire to go to America. He was, however, - sentenced to death, and the troops were actually under arms to attend his execution when a reprieve arrived. This escape was attributable to the influence exercised by the condemned man's brother, who was a medical gentleman of repute in Newtownards, and a yeoman of distinguished loyalty.

End of the Trouble.

The victory at Ballynahinch put an end to the rebellion in the North. The people, having seen their folly, returned to their homes and their industry. A common saying among the inhabitants of the Ards, for many years after, was that nobody could ever prevail on them again to attempt catching cannon balls on the prongs of pitch forks or the points of pikes.

The work of restoring peace was completed by courts-martial, executions, and banishments. Thousands of insurgents sought protections, and obtained them on taking the following oath:
> "I, --- , do solemnly promise and swear that I will bear true allegiance to his Majesty King George the Third, his heirs and successors; and I do hereby renounce and abjure all oaths and engagements of every kind whatsoever, which are in any degree contrary thereto. So help me God."

It has been stated by some that Antrim and Down were the only counties in Ulster where revolutionary ideas had a hold upon the community; but this does not represent the real condition of affairs in that province. The Roman Catholic population, with few exceptions, were in sympathy with their co-religionists in the South and West, and many members of the Protestant Churches, particularly those who had been the victims of oppressive legislation, appeared only too ready to join them and strike for home and liberty. No one will seek to justify men in rising in revolt against their rightful Sovereign, but it can, at least, be urged in extenuation of the extremes to which Nonconformists, in particular, went when associated with the United movement, that their action was the inevitable result of long-continued exasperation. Scotsmen and Englishmen, sent over to settle in uncongenial surroundings, had converted by their enterprise and industry barren wastes into fruitful fields, and opened up successful branches of trade with the most distant parts of the Empire, and yet, owing to the stupid policy which prevailed in those days, they and their children were treated as slaves of the worst class, men and women who had no claim whatever to exercise the ordinary rights of citizenship in matters either sacred or profane.

It was no wonder, then, that, trampled upon at every turn, they determined to assert their own manhood and humiliate those whom they looked upon as their persecutors. The pity, however, is that they allowed themselves to enter into alliance with people whose aims, while common in one sense, in the end could only, if successful, impose upon them a still greater bondage. Afterwards, when too late, this unnatural friendship was found out to be a mistake, and it is better, having regard to the present spirit of toleration and mutual goodwill that has sprung up in a more enlightened age, to let the matter rest there.

It has, however, to be said that the best guarantee of peace in any community, or State, is the fullest enjoyment of personal liberty consistent with the common welfare. Had the Protestant sects recognized this principle when any of them was in ascendancy, and had Rome been content with stopping there when the manacles were struck off her own supporters in Ireland, there would never have been an event so foolish and regrettable in the history of our country as the '98 rebellion. But distrust, prejudice, and love of lordship were at work, and that vile trinity could only be placated with one kind of sacrifice - the calamities of civil strife, and the horrors of religious massacre.